Don't Castrate Your Kid

A better way to handle gender confusion

Jule P. Miller III, MD

www.drjule.com

ISBN:1537660616
ISBN-13:978-1537660615

MilRose
Biloxi, MS

To My Patients

About the author

Jule P. Miller III, M.D. is the author of *Using Self Psychology in Child Psychotherapy*. He is a member of the American Academy of Child and Adolescent Psychiatry. He was Chief of Children's Mental Health at Keesler Air Force Base, medical director for two partial hospital programs for adults, and medical director for Mississippi's state run residential treatment center for delinquent teenagers. He has been seeing both adults and children as outpatients for over twenty-five years. He is in private practice in child, adolescent, and adult psychiatry in Biloxi, Mississippi.

Table of Contents

Introduction

Sometimes it seems we have woken in a parallel dimension where people have lost the capacity for common sense, where madness rules. Who would have imagined a universe where children are mutilated because of a psychiatric problem? Where teenagers beg to have their sex organs cut away and society plies them with hormones while sharpening its knives? In any normal universe it would have taken someone like Josef Mengle to imagine such a thing.

To add insult to injury, it is illegal in a number of states for mental health professionals to treat the root of the psychological problem, leaving surgery and hormones as the only options available.

Parenting is the hardest job there is. It is normal to feel anxious, to look for guidance. But there are a lot of snake-oil salesmen out there. Many of them seem respectable. Some are doctors. Some work in the government. And if we listen to them and follow what they say, it can ruin our children's lives. Above all, we need to use common sense. When "expert" opinion flies in the face of common sense, we should question it.

Does it make sense to think a three-year-old knows better what gender he is than his parent? Does it make sense that teenagers, people who typically have concerns about their changing bodies and normally go through a period of not liking different parts of their bodies, should be supported in pursuing genital mutilation and sterilization? Does it make sense that we are treating what is so obviously a psychiatric disorder with surgery?

The last time psychiatric problems were treated surgically did not work out well. The surgical procedure became widely accepted in the 1940s and 50s and was believed by some to be almost a miracle cure. The creator of the technique actually won the Nobel prize. That surgery was the lobotomy. By the time we realized it was causing more harm than benefit, tens of thousands of people in America had been lobotomized.

We are in a similar situation now. Popular culture has been falling in love with the idea that a man can become a woman, a woman a man, that there are no limits, and that the people who chose to "change sex" are pioneers rather than mentally ill. Like cheering on the alcoholic and buying him more drinks, we give transsexuals exactly what they ask for and they thank us. We leave the bar, counting their gratitude as evidence we have done a good thing, not bothering to find out that a few years down the line they are dead in the gutter. Or like a "friend" agreeing that a 75 lb adolescent anorexic girl really is "fat" and helping her find new ways to lose weight. We are enabling mental illness.

The problem with enabling this particular mental illness is that it has severe consequences. Every parent who thinks it is cute their child likes to cross-dress, or who believes they should not stand in the way of their child "finding himself," risks condemning that child to a life of infertility, expensive hormones, and dangerous surgery. Worse yet, they fix a permanent state of confusion in the child's mind, which poisons the child day and night, leading to increased substance abuse, anxiety, depression, and ultimately suicide.

If you don't want that for your child, if you want to truly help your child, then you need to ignore the media's current glamorization of transsexuals.

Overview

Gender identity disorder, gender confusion, and transgenderism all refer to the same thing: Individuals born male or female who believe they should be or are the other sex. This causes significant psychological distress. Young children with gender confusion are teased and bullied by their peers. The inner psychological conflict between their physical gender and psychological gender is a constant burden, which takes its toll on self-esteem, self-image, and general happiness. In the past this was considered a serious psychiatric disorder. In some ways it resembles a psychotic delusion. In other ways it is similar to something called body dysmorphic disorder. Then the transsexual movement gained political power and began changing social thinking. Now transgender advocates claim they do not have a disorder at all, just an alternative way of being, much like some advocates for the deaf claim they are not disabled.

Yet studies reveal that the transgender population

has a much higher incidence of psychopathology then the average individual. Personality disorders, depression, anxiety, substance abuse, and suicide are all risks of gender identity disorder. Although some people explain this in terms of the discrimination transgenders face in society, there is no evidence this is the primary determining factor. Yet activists persist in the notion that if we only stop discriminating against people with gender confusion, then they will be happy and will have essentially normal lives. This seems as much a delusion as the belief that they were somehow born the wrong sex.

But that is what our society has been moving toward, especially recently. Health insurances companies are being pressured to cover sexual reassignment surgery, first mutilating the genitals and then fashioning something vaguely resembling the anatomy of the opposite sex. Teenagers, and the push is for individuals of younger and younger age, are first put on treatments to block their natural hormones, then they are given the hormones of the opposite sex.

Whether a child likes his or her body is now considered grounds for chemically and surgically modifying that body. This is in spite of the commonly known fact that adolescents often have very ambivalent feelings about their changing bodies, that adolescence is inherently awkward, and that most teenagers grow into their adult bodies even if they suffer some initial shock during the changes. Amazingly, in several states the only "treatments" allowed are physical solutions for what is essentially a psychological problem. Psychological solutions, correcting the underlying gender identity problem, are explicitly forbidden.

It flies in the face of common sense to recommend genital mutilation for a psychological problem. Yet that is what more and more of our authorities are recommending. We have to wonder: Is there any science behind their recommendations? What assumptions is society making? And is there any evidence the treatments work?

Let us begin by looking at the assumptions behind society's ways of dealing with gender confusion. The first assumption is that gender confusion is inborn. That is, you are essentially getting a girl's brain in a boy's body or a boy's brain in a girl's body. As we will see, there is no evidence to support this. Yet we often hear the media report this assumption as if it is a proven fact. Some scientists commit the same error, sacrificing scientific integrity to support their politics.

Another assumption is that psychological treatments do not work. We will see this is incorrect as well. Although psychological treatments are more difficult the older a person gets, they are very effective in the preschool and early school years and can be helpful in the teenage years if there is enough motivation. One of the problems, however, is motivation, as teenage and adult transsexuals are typically fixated on the magical promise that hormones and surgery can "fix" them. So they often refuse the psychological help they really need. This makes them difficult to work with. That work is made even harder when our culture undercuts the validity of psychiatric care in general and glamorizes surgery. Psychotherapy takes time and involves facing difficult feelings and thoughts. It does not offer a magical cure, but a long, painful road to healing. An important point, though, is that the long road is real and leads to a fulfilling life.

The surgeons and endocrinologists who work with transsexuals promise a quick fix. But do they deliver? As we will see, there have been few long-term follow-up studies of sexual reassignment surgery. In the short term, most people say they feel better. But the only well-done, long-term study found that the older people got, the more problems they had. In particular, the other psychiatric issues were not fixed by the surgery. Ten years out, the suicide rate among people who had the surgery, and theoretically should have felt much less stressed, was many times above normal. (Dhejne, C. et al 2011).

A fundamental question is, given the high psychiatric comorbidity in transgender disorder, are we ignoring the more significant problems, the ones that lead to suicide later in life, by focusing so much on gender? Are we doing a disservice by granting surgery, often paying for it with our health insurance premiums, when it does not fix the main issues? And finally, even if surgery was helpful for some people in a number of ways, does that mean we should stop looking for psychological treatments, putting all transsexuals under the knife with the risks that entails?

To answer these questions we will look at the evidence, much of which will be taken from scientific studies published in mainstream peer-reviewed journals. I have included a list of references at the end so you can look the studies up yourself and confirm what I am saying. It is important not to blindly trust experts but to check their work, at least a sample of it, especially regarding recommendations that so profoundly affect our children.

Chapter 1: Prevalence

Transsexualism is increasing like a fire gone out of control. Although some might argue this is due to greater social acceptance, the rate of increase is too great for that explanation to hold. And what is worse, there is no sign this increase is slowing. If anything, it is accelerating.

Ann Lawrence (2008) reviewed the prevalence data from the 1960s. Back then the prevalence of male to female (MtF) transsexuals was .003% to .001%, and female to male (FtM) transsexuals had a prevalence rate of .001% to .00025%. In 2008 Lawrence cited rates corresponding to .008% of MtF and .003% for female to male transsexuals who were either on hormone therapy or had sexual reassignment surgery (SRS). She estimated that looking at all the data, the prevalence of transsexuality had increased by a factor of 10.

In 2011 Gary J. Gates of the Williams Institute at

UCLA Law School looked at nine surveys that had been done in the seven years leading up to his report. He found that the prevalence of people who identify as transgender was .3%. If you notice, that is 100 times the number Lawrence gave for FtM transsexuals in 2008.

In June of 2016 the Williams Institute released another report, this one titled, "How Many Adults Identify as Transgender in the United States?" This report utilized the CDC's Behavioral Risk Factor Surveillance System to estimate the percentage and number of adults who identify as transgender nationally and in all 50 states based on survey data taken in 19 states. This is the largest survey that has ever been done in the USA. Nationally, .6% of people surveyed said they were transgender (roughly 60 times higher than the MtF rates of Lawrence and 200 times the FtM rate she quoted). The state data ranged from a low of .3% in North Dakota to a high of .8% in Hawaii. Comparing different age groups in each state revealed that the youngest group surveyed, 18 to 24 years-old, had the highest prevalence of transgenderism at .7%, while those over 65 had a rate of .5%.

There are two important points from this most recent survey. One is that the prevalence numbers are much higher than the numbers Lawrence quoted. Another is that the findings support the view that the incidence of transgenderism is increasing. This is further buttressed by the fact that the younger age group shows the highest prevalence, demonstrating that the expansion of gender confusion is continuing.

It is not just in America that the prevalence of transgender cases has been increasing. Kenneth J. Zucker, who ran a premier gender clinic for children and adolescents in Toronto before it was shut down late in 2015 by radical trans-activists, reported in

2014 that "the number of referred adolescent cases has increased dramatically over the past 8 years, with an almost fivefold increase in annual referrals from prior years." Cecilia Dhejne (2014) in looking at all applications for sex reassignment surgery in Sweden from 1960 to 2010 reported a tripling of applications from 1972 to 2010, with the most pronounced increase after 2000. Clearly, this is a growing problem.

A question that immediately comes to mind is, why are the numbers for transgender disorder increasing so dramatically? As I mentioned, one possible explanation is that society is now more accepting of gender variations. Transgender characters are increasingly seen on television and the movies. The federal government has included transgenderism as a civil right protected under title IX. So there is a surface appeal to the idea that the actual number of transgender individuals is not increasing so much as that more people are willing to admit it now. Yet the enormity of the increase, 200 times greater in comparing the latest Williams Institute figures to Lawrence's, is too great to be explained by this; it simply does not make common sense. It defies reason. So what is causing the increase?

The increase in gender confusion closely parallels the breakdown of society's clear gender roles. The feminist revolution has had positive effects that are well documented, such as increased job opportunities for women, but it also caused dramatic changes in child-rearing. The well defined arrangement of the past 100,000 years where women raised the children until the boys were old enough to hunt, farm, or go to school, a system marked by stability and predictability, has been replaced by multiple and frequently changing caretakers, a chaotic schedule, and parents, when they are available, often bringing their stress home with them. Rules have been cast aside, leading to confusion and stress. It is no wonder there is more gender confusion – there is more confusion overall.

Besides the general stresses I mentioned, parents no longer have clear guideposts on how to raise a child. There are too many opinions, too many people telling them anything goes. Society used to agree and be very clear on how children should be raised and treated. The dark side of the multiple social revolutions that began in the 60's and 70's is a loss of coherence and any sort of reliable guide.

Toddlers work hard to figure out the rules. They play out the various possibilities. They are not helped when no one sets limits or guides them. Without those limits they become confused and anxious. Gender confusion can often be reined in when it first appears at age 2 or 3, but parents have come to believe they should not interfere with the "natural unfolding" of their child's development, rather than realizing they are an important part of shaping that development, whether they like it or not.

It is because these problems are not dealt with early that we have teenagers wanting to take hormones and have surgeries, forever destroying their fertility and putting themselves at huge risk. It is because there is no early intervention and treatment that these children go through years of peer alienation. It is because nothing is done that children must struggle with a burdensome inner conflict they should not have to deal with. Is it any surprise that transgender youth and adults have significantly higher rates of depression, anxiety, suicide, and substance abuse?

If I am right, and more people are actually suffering from gender confusion than in the past, then it will only get worse. This is because society has bought into the transgender lobby's brainwashing and political pressure and now believes that psychological gender is inborn and unchangeable in spite of the fact that science recognizes that every other aspect of humanity is malleable and results from a combination of genes and environment. It is now politically incorrect and professionally dangerous to say anything that contradicts the party line. And it is illegal to offer therapy to treat gender identity disorder in children in a number of states. What worked for tens of thousands of years is being disregarded, replaced by the pathological ideas of a small number, and we are enabling this.

Personally, I am all for acceptance and love, but I do not want the government telling me how to raise my child and whether it is permissible for me to get help for my 3 year-old son who says he wants to have his penis cut off so he can be like his sister. I don't want him to go to nursery school and be shown a cartoon about a boy happily changing into a girl. I don't want him to suffer the taunts and jeers of other children when he reaches grade school. I don't want him to feel confused about who he is or what he is to the point where he may someday not want to live anymore. I don't want him to willingly surrender his reproductive potential and the body parts he was born with all for the sake of an illusion. I want a normal son who grows up to give me grandchildren. If he has issues with his sense of self, whether it is his gender or self-esteem or any other aspect of who he is, I want to be able to get him the help he needs so he can learn to accept and love who he is.

Imagine for a moment a society of teenagers who don't know if they are boys or girls, or whether they will end up as men or women. That is not freedom; that is pathetic. Being an adolescent is hard enough without having to worry about what sex you are. Why do we put that burden on them when we can fix it when they are young? Why do we let it go on? Why don't we work at finding real treatment, psychological treatment, to help them adjust to who they are biologically, because that is a lot of what childhood and adolescence is about anyway – adjusting to your body at each point in its development.

The toddler has to come to terms with his small size and relative weakness. He has to learn to depend on his parents rather than fight them with tantrums; he needs their protection and provision. He has to learn to put off his wishes to rule the roost until he can have a family of his own. The school age child has to adapt to the different rates of maturation of his or her body compared to peers. She has to accept that she will not be the fastest, strongest, or tallest. And going through puberty, the teenager has to get used to huge changes in his body, voice, and mind. It is not easy. Many teenagers have a hard time of it. A final adult sense of self is not possible for most people in today's culture until the early twenties.

Proponents of sexual reassignment surgery will argue that postponing hormones and surgery until after adolescence makes the transition harder; the changes wrought by puberty leave an indelible mark on the body that will interfere with the process of changing sex. To a degree they are right, but that is assuming the transition cannot be prevented. I would rather help an individual adjust his inner perception, something that all teens have to do, than wrench his body through chemical changes and physical mutilation. We will look at the evidence later about how well treatment of all kinds fares in this group.

Most people with gender identity disorder remember feeling different since childhood, although it typically becomes much more intense with puberty.

Thus, in almost all cases it is potentially identifiable at an early age. While psychological treatment is more problematic in adolescence or adulthood, it is often successful in childhood. In general, the younger the child, the more likely psychological treatment will work.

Chapter 2: Comorbidity

What is often not discussed when talking about transsexualism is how ill transgender people typically are. Depression, anxiety, personality disorders, and substance abuse are the norm. There have been a number of studies that cherry picked only the healthiest transsexuals for sexual reassignment surgery. Not surprisingly, those studies show that the carefully selected group, evaluated by a paper and pen test that is no substitute for an in-depth clinical interview, appear otherwise healthy before and after surgery. But they are not typical.

A 2005 study in the Journal of Psychosomatic Research looked at 31 patients undergoing or who had recently undergone sexual reassignment surgery and assessed them with a standard research test, the SCID. They found that 42% of the patients had at least one personality disorder, 39% had a current Axis I psychiatric disorder (a psychiatric disorder typically treated with medication), and 71% had a current or lifetime Axis I disorder. These numbers are way above what you find in the normal population (comorbidity GID Hepp 2005). Adding Axis I and Axis II reveals that 81% of the patients had a current psychiatric disorder in addition to transsexualism. One thing that should be kept in mind is that all of these individuals had to go through a psychiatric assessment before being accepted for surgery, so they represent the best case scenario.

Surgery advocates say the reason for the high incidence of other psychiatric disorders is due to the internal distress of being born in the wrong body. According to them, once surgery and hormones renders physical appearance consistent with psychological gender, then all that misery should go away, right? Wrong.

The only way to really know how people do is to follow them over the long term. Immediately after this kind of surgery most people will understandably be ecstatic with finally getting what they wanted. The reality has to have time to sink in. Unfortunately, almost all the studies purporting to show positive results for sexual reassignment surgery consist of asking patients how they feel about it immediately or shortly after surgery. There is almost no long-term data. I say almost, because there is exactly one top quality long-term follow-up study of sexual reassignment surgery. It was published in 2011 by a Swedish group that followed all 324 sex-reassigned persons in Sweden from 1973-2003, matched by birth year and birth sex to random population controls. (Dhejne, C. et al, 2011).

What they found was the further out in time you looked, the worse the trans group did compared to the normal population. Further, the overall suicide rate was 19 times higher than the normal population – and this is in the group that got what they wanted: the surgery. They were also almost 3 times as likely to be hospitalized on a psychiatric ward, and the female to male transsexuals had a higher rate of criminal convictions. Yet, we are led to believe that transsexuals only have gender issues and are otherwise normal. We are further asked to believe that surgery will fix their psychological problems – with a 19 fold risk of suicide, I would say not.

Chapter 3: Causes

Biological

The biggest lie of the transgender movement is that gender identity disorder is the result of being born with the brain of the opposite sex. This is known as the biological theory: there was a genetic problem, or the fetus's brain was exposed to the wrong hormones at the wrong time (although how and why this would happen inside the womb is always left out), or there were some adverse hormone exposures shortly after birth that "feminized" the boy's brain or "androgenized" the girl's brain.

Rubbish. Sure, you can give pregnant rats a big shot of testosterone and it will affect her female offspring's behavior; so what? There is no evidence anything like that has happened to transgender humans, unless you suspect their mothers as being pro-body-builders. Didn't happen.

There are some natural experiments that are use-

ful to look at. One is where females are born with
with congenital adrenal hyperplasia (CAH), a disorder where the adrenal glands produce excessive
amounts of male hormones (androgens). The excess
of male hormones masculinizes the little girl's genitals, making them appear to some extent male. Mild
cases are usually recognized early, and treatments to
suppress the excess hormones and surgery to femi-
nize the genitals can allow these children to have relatively normal lives as girls and women. Some more
severe cases are   mistaken for boys and raised as
such. In both cases, it is presumed that the child's
brain was immersed in male hormones during gesta-
tion. So what happens to these children? Do the girls
have boy brains?

Arianne Dessens and colleagues from the Nether-
lands reported on a group of such children in 2005.
They looked at a number of studies, which allowed
them to pool the results of 250 children with CAH
raised as girls and 33 raised as boys. Of the 250
raised as girls, 237 did not show any symptoms of
gender dysphoria. In other words, 94.8% were happy
being female in spite of early intrauterine exposure
to male hormones. 5.25% experienced gender dysphoria, which is higher than the normal population,
but clearly demonstrates that intrauterine hormones
are not a major factor in gender identity in CAH girls.

What about the CAH children raised as males?
12.1% of those were gender dysphoric; which is in-
teresting since they, like the CAH children raised female, had been exposed to masculine hormones in
utero. So there must have been some other factor in
that small subset that led to the gender dysphoria. I
suspect the family's knowledge of the genetic gender
had an effect on the child's developing gender identity, undermining the decision to raise the child as a

male. This would be another demonstration of the power of the unconscious in families and individuals.

In any case, what is apparent is that gender identity is not fixed by intrauterine hormones. As Dessens puts it, "these observations confirm the conclusion by Hines (2004) that gender identity development, at least in patients with classical CAH, is remarkably flexible."

Another natural experiment involves biologic males who have suffered loss of their male genitalia through biological or surgical accidents and have been raised as females from an early age. These children started out with normally functioning testes but had them removed sometime after birth in order to facilitate development as females. In 2005 Heino Meyer-Bahlburg from Columbia University published a review of the literature regarding the outcome of such children.

In an important way this population is more psychologically difficult for parents than in the case of girls with CAH. Typically, girls with CAH are raised successfully as girls. There might be the need for some surgical repair work, and there is the need for medication to keep the symptoms of CAH at bay during development, but the parents get a daughter who is raised as a daughter. Parents of boys who because of biological accident (penile agenesis, cloacal exstrophy of the bladder, and classical exstrophy of the bladder) or physical accidents (surgical errors, dog bites, etc.) are faced with the decision to fully castrate their child, removing functioning testes in order to salvage what they can from a horrible situation. There can be no doubt that many such parents never fully let go of the son who almost was. Many must feel castration guilt. Although on the surface they may seem to have come to terms with what life has dealt, what goes on in their unconscious is another thing entirely.

Consequently, we might expect the ghost of the boy-who-was to inhabit the parent-child relationship. We would predict that the attempt to transform the damaged boy into a functional girl might not be quite as effective as 95% of CAH girls being able to maintain their female gender identity. So what are the results? Across all ages, 78% were still living as females. If you subtracted those with gender dysphoria, the number is 65% living as females and content with their gender. Obviously not as high as the girls with CAH, but still the majority.

It may be that intrauterine hormones have some effect on gender identity, but there is no clear evidence. What is apparent is that the effect, if it exists, is a minor effect, and that other factors are more important. There is more evidence that intrauterine hormones have an impact on activity level and type of play, but this is a different matter and does not appear to be directly related to gender identity except as a factor that might interact with other determinants.

So even in these extreme cases of biological error, the effect of early life hormone imbalance is not a deal breaker as far as gender identity. And there is no evidence the vast majority of transgender individuals had any hormone abnormality at any time of their life.

Let us look at some of the other biological arguments in more depth. The first is the genetic one. It is primarily based on the fact that a greater number of identical twins than fraternal twins share gender confusion. Supposedly this shows that since identical twins share all their DNA and fraternal twins just half, the difference must be genetic. But this disregards the fact that most identical twins are reared more similarly than fraternal twins. Parents like to dress their identical twins the same, other children tend to treat them the same, and they often develop a special closeness early in life. In other words, not only are identical twins more closely related biologically, they are closer in family environment as well. Fraternal twins, unlike identical twins, can even be of the opposite sex.

So what do the studies say? One study by Gunter Heylens out of Belgium was published in 2012 in the Journal of Sexual Medicine. He reviewed 23 monozygotic twin pairs and 21 dizygotic twin pairs in which at least one twin had gender identity disorder. He found that the concordance rate for the 23 monozygotic twins in his study was 39.1% while none of the 21 dizygotic twins were concordant. To me there are several things to be learned from this. One is that these results cast further doubt on the intrauterine hormone hypothesis. All of the twins, monozygotic and dizygotic, would share in the same maternal hormonal environment and may also influence one another through a prenatal transfer of hormones from one twin to the other. Yet none of the 21 dizygotic twins shared their siblings' gender issues. So what happened to the hormone effect? If intrauterine hormones were crucial in causing gender dysphoria, we would expect to see a significant concordance between dizygotic twins as well.

This kind of result is what we expect when the bias of the researchers is taken out of the equation. All researchers hope to prove something. Typically, they manage to find evidence to support their pet theory. By looking at the data in a way that they did not intend, in a way that was not affected by their bias, you might find less tainted evidence. This has been done in studies comparing old and new antidepressants. Invariably the authors want to show the new antidepressant works well. They don't care so much how the old antidepressant performs. And so it is not uncommon for the study to show that the new antidepressant separates from placebo while the old one does not, inadvertently casting doubt on the whole category of medication. In this case, the lack of any concordance among the dizygotic twins is a powerful rebuttal to the intrauterine hormone hypothesis.

60.9% of monozygotic twins were discordant. That means that even if genetic factors are important, they are in the minority. And the fact that identical twins lead unusually similar early lives makes the 39.1% concordance rate understandable from a purely environmental explanation. So how much is really due to genetics? We don't know; the evidence simply does not exist. One thing for sure, if there is a genetic effect, it is relatively small.

Another argument for the genetics of gender confusion is that there is a higher incidence of gender problems in the first degree relatives of transsexuals than there is in the general population. This is just another variation of the twin theme, and the same argument of family members sharing an environment can be used here.

It is important to note that I am not saying there are no genetic contributions to gender dysphoria whatsoever, just that we have no proof that they exist, and if they do, they are less significant than early childhood experiences and are more likely along the line of temperamental variables, such as a heightened sensitivity to stimuli or a tendency to anxiety, which influences the child's reactions to his environment. An example of this would be a boy who is born with a very sensitive temperament. The rough and tumble play of other boys might feel overwhelming to him. The quieter, gentler play of girls might fit his temperament better, leading him to play preferentially with girls. This is one factor among many that can then influence which sex he identifies with. If he happens to have a father who is similar in temperament, the natural fit between them will tend to counteract peer influences. If his parents find male playmates who are also less rambunctious, this will help. As he grows up, rather than sports he might gravitate to the arts or intellectual activities and identify with famous male artists and thinkers. Or he might take up golf or chess, sports that are decidedly not rambunctious. Then again, with time and encouragement he may grow out of his shell and become more outgoing.

The effect of temperament can be limited and overcome by learning. The introvert can learn to be a great actor, even a politician. The extrovert can learn to enjoy quiet, solitary activities. And those boys who initially feel more at home playing with girls may find that by the time they are in high school they are playing basketball with the rest of the guys.

Finally, there is the brain. A number of studies purport to show that the brains of male to female transgenders resemble female brains, while the brains of female to male transgenders resemble male brains. First, as someone who actually looks at brain scans, I can tell you that there is no way to tell if a brain is male or female by just looking at it. There was a recent article that emphasized this by describing individual brains as having a "mosaic" of what have been classically described as male and female parts rather than fitting one stereotype or the other (Joel, D., et al. 2015).

Does that mean there are no gender based brain differences? Looking at large groups of brains can give you general ideas of differences, but that does not let you classify any individual. In other words, the differences are not remarkable or evident to anyone but a statistician with a powerful computer. And even then, they are questionable.

But what finally causes us to pitch all these studies out the window is that we now know brain structures change, they grow bigger or smaller, depending on experience. This has been famously demonstrated in the case of London cabbies who have to learn all the streets and stops in London to do their job. Their brains have been studied at the beginning and end of their training, and remarkable alterations of size have occurred in their hippocampi, a part of the brain intimately tied to memory. (Woollett, K. 2011). These physical changes are far beyond the differences researchers describe for transsexuals, and they were created by only four years of experience. Now imagine for a moment what 10 or more years of thinking and acting like the opposite sex might do to your brain.

In support of the idea that experience is the most important factor in causing any difference between the brains of transsexuals and normal people is that these supposed differences are not visible in the brains of children (Chung W. 2002). So the most plausible explanation for any neuroanatomic differences is experience.

You can see it is not hard to refute the arguments that transgenderism has much to do with biology. I could spend many more pages taking apart each argument, each study that purports to show transgenderism is biologically determined. But I am more interested in telling you what does cause gender dysphoria and what to do to help. Having actually read the studies others reference, I can tell you that there is no proof gender dysphoria has a primary genetic or hormonal basis. There is nothing to the idea of being born with the wrong brain. Despite this, the majority of scientific and popular press publications claim it is all about biology. That should tell you something about the relative power of emotions and politics versus rational thought, reason, and science, even among scientists.

So if the predominant cause of transgenderism is not biology, though it plays a role in laying down vulnerabilities to certain kinds of stress, than what is? There are three main causes: culture, family interactions, and the child's inner experience. The scientific support for these arguments will broaden to include the psychoanalytic literature. To understand why, we must take a moment, get philosophical, and consider the nature of proof.

Proof

How do we know what goes on in the minds of young children? Is there an X-ray of the mind? Is there a psychological test we can use to probe gender formation? No. But there is a way of directly observing the phenomena under question.

The only way we have survived as a species against the many predators who are much stronger and fiercer than Man has been through cooperation. Evolution has made us above all social animals, and as a part of that social design, our brains are hardwired for empathy.

Empathy is quite literally the ability to enter someone else's mind. There have been numerous studies that have demonstrated that from infancy on we have the capacity to feel what another is feeling just by observing his facial expressions and body language.

Brain scans of two individuals, one experiencing a powerful emotion and the other watching, will reveal the observer's brain replicating the same pattern of neural activity as the observed's brain. Other scientists have identified particular "mirror neurons" that are active in the brain of a person doing a particular task. Those same neurons are active in the brain of someone imagining doing the task and in the brain of someone watching the first person do the task. We are designed to share feeling states and to be able to imagine ourselves into our fellow human beings' thoughts. In other words, we are all born mind readers.

Empathy gives us a natural route to enter the minds of children and see for ourselves what is going on during development. Heinz Kohut, in a 1959 paper on empathy, remarked that, "the inner world cannot be observed with the aid of our sensory organs. Our thoughts, wishes, feelings, and fantasies cannot be seen, smelled, heard, or touched. They have no existence in physical space, and yet they are real, and we can observe them as they occur in time: through introspection in ourselves, and through empathy (i.e., vicarious introspection) in others." (Kohut, 1959). The training and experience of psychoanalytic therapists sharpens and extends their empathy, allowing them to see things the average person could not. Their empathy has become a finally tuned instrument.

Psychoanalytic therapists of young children have the same advantage that Antonie van Leeuwenoek had in the 1600's with his early microscope – they can see the evidence for what they are talking about, just as Leeuwenhoek could see his "animalcules" in a drop of water. He was the first one to view bacteria, as well as many other microscopic items of interest, but initially was not believed by the Royal Society when he claimed to see a single-cell organism. Because he was the only one with the microscope lenses capable of this magnification, members of the Royal Society had to come to him to look through his microscope and verify his findings.

Being an expert is psychoanalytic psychotherapy is similar to being one of the few people with a working microscope in the 1600's. Except the microscope needed to verify the claims of psychoanalytic work cannot be bought. Instead, a person has to spend years of training and practice to become the microscope. It is no wonder, I suppose, that some people doubt what they cannot see, just as the Royal Society at first doubted Leeuwenhoek. Although in some ways the situation is more difficult than in the 1600's as there is no microscope a lay person can look through, in another way it is better as there are and have been many trained "microscopes," both now and in the past 100 years, who have written of their observations.

Those observations are typically discounted by people who rely on statistics and "objective" psychological testing, but the fact is that the only ones with access to the best data concerning gender development are psychoanalytic therapists of children. There is no other way to see bacteria than through a microscope, or the rings of Saturn than through a telescope; statistics and pen and paper tests are irrelevant. It would be like the Royal Society trying to judge Leeuwenhoek's work by tasting the water or measuring the size of the drop.

Kohut remarked: "Valid scientific research in psychoanalysis is nevertheless possible because (1) the empathic understanding of the experiences of other human beings is as basic an endowment of man as his vision, hearing, touch, taste, and smell; and (2) psychoanalysis can deal with the obstacles that stand in the way of empathic comprehension just as other sciences have learned to deal with the obstacles that stood in the way of mastering the use of the observational tools – sensory organs, including their extension and refinement through instruments – they employed." (Kohut 1977).

So what does our psychological "microscope" reveal?

Inner Experience

As almost all infants and toddlers are taken care of by women, either the mother or her substitute during the day, it is fair to say that the infant's first love as well as first model for identification, whether that infant is a boy or a girl, is the mother. Hence, both boys and girls begin with a female gender identification, and boys and girls both love women first.

For the boy, gender identity is more complicated than in girls. Both start with a female identification, but boys have to switch to a male identification. On the contrary, sexual orientation is harder for the girl, as she has to switch from the strong love she feels for her mother to a love of men. These complementary difficulties are reflected in the higher rate of men applying for sexual reassignment surgery and the greater sexual fluidity of women.

For the boy the process of changing to a masculine gender begins when he starts to walk away from his mother. The new toddler relishes the feeling of power, of being able to do things, as he pulls the dog's ears, turns the cable box off, throws things, and runs laughing out into the street, chased by his screaming parents. He becomes intoxicated with the power of it all. His mother is terrified and generally tries to restrict his actions. His father, however, has mixed feelings, and is more likely to amplify his son's feelings by throwing him up in the air, rolling around with him on the floor, and chasing him, both laughing, through the house, much to the mother's exasperation at her husband's "childish" antics. But those antics are a key ingredient in helping children, boys and girls, separate from their mother. During this time both sexes fall in love with their father.

The time from two to five years of age is the most imaginative time of human existence. During this time the child is literally creating the core of who he will be for the rest of his life. As an infant his sense of self was intimately dependent on his relationship with his caregivers. Now the second half of his "psychological skeleton," the structure around which he will organize all the rest of his experience, is created by his own imagination. Yes, he is still dependent on his parents, but his developing desires, experiences, and sense of self act through his imagination to create fantasies that will become the basis for his sexual attractions later in life, for what interests him at work and in school, for how he finds meaning in the world, and for how he sees himself, including his gender identity.

Through countless interactions, the majority occurring on an unconscious level, boys' and girls' early experiences shape their fantasies, so boys end up switching their identifications to their fathers and girls end up wanting to marry someone just like him when they grow up. This is helped, I imagine, by biological imperatives or the human race would not have survived for long, which goes to show that for true gender confusion to develop, there must be some major psychological problems in the first years of life. However, since those problems most likely were only evident in the fantasies the two to five year-old created, and since most parents are not aware of their child's fantasies, and most children cannot recall them after they reach school age, the evidence is lost.

But it is not lost to child therapists who have the training and ability to observe the fantasies developing and changing in their consulting room.

By five years of age the child has developed a set of fantasies that help explain his place in the world and give him a guide to his future. In some children the fantasies are not well adapted to reality. When a boy's psychological work results in a belief that he is really a girl, he suffers a profound inner conflict. There are then only two possible solutions: change his body to match his mind or change his mind to match his body. The origins and nature of the problematic fantasies, however, are unconscious by the time he reaches puberty. To his conscious recollection he has always felt this way and there seems no other obvious explanation than that he was born wrong, which leaves surgery as the magic solution.

Another reason transsexuals do not accept a psychological explanation for their problems, besides the fact that the evidence is now unconscious, is they usually have strong unconscious motivations to avoid looking at their thoughts and feelings too closely. The surgical solution is part of their denial. Looking inward is threatening in that it brings individuals face to face with anxiety, shame, and rage: things they do not want to experience. So they turn to surgery instead. But as we have seen from the long-term Swedish study, the procedure is not magical, and after an initial feeling of hope and triumph the old feelings reveal themselves, despair sets in, and then suicide.

Culture and Parenting

As the child grows, culture is transmitted through the relationships he experiences. If the pre-K teacher tells her three-year-old students they don't have to be boys or girls if they don't want to, she has dropped a depth charge into the children's developing unconscious. If a four-year-old goes to school to find his best friend is now wearing girl's clothes, and the teacher insists the child is a girl, his confusion may go beyond the bounds he can handle.

It is hard at first for a child in a bilingual household, but they come out the better for it. In the same way, a child brought up with a father and mother has to learn to "speak" male and female. That can be confusing enough, but as long as the grammar and vocabulary remain distinct and clear, the result is a more well-rounded person. If the grammar and vocabulary of what is male and what is female becomes mixed up, messy, then it is hard to learn any language at all, and the child is the worse for it.

Which brings me to parenting. Many of us have been influenced by the feminist revolution to believe children should have an equal vote with their parents on virtually all issues. We have been taught that gender roles are socially constructed and somehow bad.

Gender roles are partly socially constructed, but they are not bad, they serve a very real purpose. As I just described with my analogy to learning a language, there need to be clear rules. Without them the child is handicapped in her learning.

As we have allowed society to tell us we should not instill gender stereotypes in our children, we have left them nothing to hold onto and learn from. It is all a confusing mess. No wonder the incidence of transgenderism is dramatically increasing. That increase really took off around 2000, when the people born in the 60's, 70's, and 80's became old enough and rich enough to afford surgery. The same decades that up-ended society spawned the rapid rise in gender confusion. This is not a sign of a morally superior society working to end discrimination; it is a sign of disorganization and chaos, an indicator of the breakdown of one aspect of civilization.

Finally, the influence of parents is paramount to gender identity. Often it is possible to see one or both parents playing into and reinforcing the cross-gender role. Sometimes this is done consciously, but most often unconsciously. Sometimes the mother really needs her son to be a little girl. Sometimes the father wants a son and his daughter accommodates. Sometimes the girl's envy of her father's power becomes an identification, and her parents may not know how to provide her with an alternative way of handling her need for power that does not involve a cross-gender identification. Sometimes a boy may so idolize his older sister that he wants to be her, and his mother thinks it is cute and admires his "going against the flow." Generally, helping these families involves working with the parents as well as the child.

Chapter 4: Treatments

Because of the mistaken belief that people are born with a fixed psychological gender that is immune to all attempts to change, the current recommendations for treating gender dysphoria involve adapting the body and the environment to fit the pathological belief. This means starting treatment to halt puberty either early in puberty or, increasingly, before puberty has begun. This is followed by administering cross-gender sex hormones during puberty, followed by surgery near the end of adolescence to remove and reshape the genitals into something vaguely resembling the opposite sex. The argument is being made more and more frequently to lower the age at which these steps are done, the idea being to prevent any trace of normal puberty so that the transition to the opposite sex will be less painful both socially and surgically. However, as we have discussed, this is all based on incorrect assumptions about gender and the capacity for young children to change.

The only psychotherapy currently being discussed involves helping the child, the family, and the community cope with the transsexual's "true" gender and the changes that the child will be going through. It is almost like the story of the Emperor's new clothes where the emperor walks around naked and everyone has to pretend he is wearing the finest clothes around. Only in this case the pretense is much more damaging.

The biggest assumption of all, and the one at the core of all this, is that you can change your sex. Surgery does not give men a real vagina or women a real penis. It gives them something that looks similar but does not work all that well. Hormone treatments and surgery are just improved versions of crossdressing, of pretend play. Nothing can change a man into a woman or visa versa. You are born one way and that is it. Anything else is a fantasy. But the medical and surgical industry has advertised this fantasy as if it were reality, thus contributing to the transsexuals' pathology, not helping them. To reiterate, a 19 fold increased suicide rate following sexual reassignment surgery – not a roaring good sign of success.

Transgenders are powerfully motivated to deny any kind of psychological treatment can help, especially with young children, because that would destroy the fantasy that they are "really" the opposite sex and can magically metamorphose through the wonders of surgery into their "real self." If, on the other hand, they are shown to be clinging to a delusion, then there is something fundamentally wrong with their minds, and that is terrifying to contemplate. What if they suddenly realize they have been fooling themselves and carrying on a big charade this whole time? What feelings are they left with then?

If the radical transsexual activists are wrong, and this is an illness that could have been fixed by psychotherapy, then all the painful surgery, long periods of recovery, physical therapy, scars and having to adapt with each surgery and hormone change would have been for nought. They will have mutilated their bodies for nothing. They will have been left with a scarred and painful crude facsimile of the opposite sex for nothing. They will have given up their fertility for nothing.

Finally, there is all the peer ostracism they went through, when they proudly proclaimed themselves the other sex. To admit they were wrong is to open the door to the social pain they locked away. They would not want to give up their victories; so they hold onto their pain and suffering as a flag of pride.

Surgical Techniques

The techniques used vary depending on whether they are meant to alter a male body to make it look more female, or a female body to look more male. In all cases we are talking about major surgery with risks of scarring, chronic pain, and death. I advise the reader to view pictures on the internet to make it all the more clear how drastic surgery on one's genitals is. For instance, here is a link to an article that gives a good description, with some pictures, of what is involved in creating a "vagina" in a man: http://www.hindawi.com/journals/tswj/2014/6389 19/. (Bizic, et al. Retrieved 8/16/2016).

The gold standard technique for male to female transsexuals involves turning the penis inside-out to make a short vagina. It begins with castrating the man by removing his testicles. Next, his penis is cut into several sections and fashioned into a tube. The surgeon creates a place for the new vagina by cutting into the patient, then fixes the inverted penis into place. The urethra, through which urine flows, has to be properly mounted or it won't work right. There remains the problem of lubrication, infections, the possibility the sutures could come loose or the vagina could prolapse (which is like a balloon turning inside out).

When the patient goes home, he has to keep dilating his new "vagina" for a number of months or it won't work properly. The size of the neovagina is limited by the amount of skin taken from the penis.

Another procedure involves taking part of the colon to create a new vagina, often in conjunction with using the skin from the penis as well. This allows greater length for the vagina, and there is a natural lubrication process (if you consider intestinal secretions an appealing sexual lubricant). It also involves less dilation.

Neither of these procedures are perfect. Neither turns a man into a woman. They have gotten better over the years. But genital flap vaginas are not as durable as real vaginas and may suffer with vigorous intercourse. Sigmoid intestine vaginas are more durable but it is possible to get colon cancer or colitis in the new vagina. All of them involve significant recovery time, pain, potential for scarring and adhesions, and the risk of infection.

Procedures for changing women into "men" are even more involved because a penis has to be simulated in some way. This involves taking a graft from somewhere else on the body. It also involves cutting away the female parts and refashioning them into a false scrotum. The uterus and ovaries are cut out. The breasts are hacked away.

The most risky part for the woman changing to a

"man" is extending the urethra. If it is not done right, it won't work, and it is relatively fragile compared to the other tissues being worked with. The other risks are similar to the male to female surgery.

Besides the surgery to the sex organs, additional surgeries are often undertaken to: insert a penile implant, shave down the Adam's apple, reshape the chest, reshape the face, etc.

In the process of all this, the chance to ever have biological children is destroyed. The body is irrevocably altered. Those individuals who try to reverse the procedure simply add more scars on top of the ones they have already.

Hormones

Before surgery, in preparation for it, and after surgery hormone treatments are the mainstay of transgender life. They allow men to grow breasts and women to grow beards. They are the next step up from just dressing like the other sex. Inevitably, transgender children want cross-gender hormones. Often, as a compromise, children just on the edge of puberty are given hormone blockers to stop puberty for a couple of years so the child can fully make up his or her mind before beginning cross-gender hormones. Then, in mid-adolescence, if the teenager is still determined to change sex, cross-sex hormones will be started.

The idea of hormone blockers may seem like a reasonable compromise between giving a young adolescent cross-gender hormones and refusing any intervention, which would force the child to at least go through the beginning of puberty, but it is actually a trap. It gives a false sense of rationality. Interfering with puberty while time goes on and peers develop is an artificial and bizarre state that in no way allows normal rational reflection and evaluation. It is not a pause to consider; it is the first step of a choice that will end in bodily mutilation, loss of fertility, and a lifelong dependence on someone else's hormones.

How many kids elect not to go forward? Once started down the road of messing with hormones, almost all follow it till the end. One study of 70 adolescents who started on puberty suppressing hormones ended with all 70 going on to sexual reassignment surgery (de Vries, A. 2011).

When children take the next step and go on cross-gender hormones, they never have the chance to adapt to the body they were born to have, which is one of the main tasks of adolescence. The psychological delusion of being born in the wrong body is given the upper hand and adaptation to reality made impossible by the family and doctor's collusion, as well as by the hijacking of the child's body and mind by cross-sex hormones. It sounds like an experiment Josef Mengele would have approved of.

Something else often overlooked is that each set of hormones carries risks. For men who want to be like women, taking estrogen increases their risks of deep vein thromboses, high blood pressure, liver abnormalities, bone problems, and strokes. Women who want to be like men may show an increased rate of criminality, heart attacks, and stroke, among other things.

The Prototypical Surgery for Psychiatric Problems

The long term follow-up study out of Sweden says: "Sex reassignment also involves the surgical removal of body parts.... This is a unique intervention not only in psychiatry but in all of medicine." (Dhejne C,

2011). To me, it resembles one other psychiatric treatment that has long been discontinued: lobotomy.

Like sexual reassignment surgery (SRS), lobotomy was a surgical solution to a mental problem. Like SRS, lobotomy was once accepted as the gold standard, the ideal treatment. It was thought to be a miracle cure for psychosis with few complications or problems. In fact, the creator of the lobotomy, Antonio Egaz Moniz, received the Nobel prize in medicine in 1949 for his creation. It was widely used for over 20 years; during that time about 40,000 patients in the United States alone had lobotomies (source: "Lobotomy" Wikipedia. Retrieved 8/28/2016).

Two things ended up stopping the use of lobotomies: over the long term it became clear that there were many adverse effects and not as many benefits as had been suggested, and better treatments, particularly antipsychotics, were developed. It can be argued that those better treatments might not have been developed if there had been a strong lobby of schizophrenics wanting lobotomies and opposing anything but surgery as being motivated by prejudice and hatred.

In comparing lobotomy to SRS, it should be kept in mind that psychosis has been a much more common event, so the problems associated with surgical treatment were likely to be seen quicker. For the same reason, there was more research being done on alternative treatments, something that may not even be possible anymore with transsexualism, given the political climate. Finally, there were about 40,000 lobotomies done in America. We do not know how many SRSs have occurred in America. We do know that in the 30 year follow-up in Sweden, it was only 324. I imagine it is much higher than that now and rising daily. I would not be surprised if we have hit the 40,000 mark in America already.

The big difference between lobotomy and SRS, however, is that patients want SRS and they do not usually want a lobotomy. What has driven all this is that the doctors, who are supposed to cure patients of their delusions, have instead become partners with the patients in supporting the delusion and validating it. "Sure, you are a girl trapped in a boy's body, we can fix that, just pull down your pants and I will get my knife." Although that sounds crude, like I am distorting reality to make a point, it is more accurate than the euphemisms and vague descriptions used by the popular press.

When lobotomies were in vogue there were no effective treatments for most major mental illnesses. It seemed to many that the benefits outweighed the drawback of spending a lifetime in a mental institution. To many transsexuals it seems the benefits of surgery, the only choice they believe they have to rid themselves of gender dysphoria, is worth the risks of surgery, sterilization, and subnormal sexual functioning for the rest of their lives. Not to mention the scaring, pain, and need for repeat procedures in an attempt to continually chase perfection. But they do have other choices, better choices, that address the psychiatric problems that cause their suffering.

There are, of course, some people whose gender disorder has been counterbalanced by such good experiences in other aspects of life that their mental health seems spared in many ways. These are the unusual cases but are the ones you tend to hear about in the news. How spared they really are, however, is open to question, as the measures researchers used to track emotional health simply do not equate to Leeuwenhoek's microscope.

Another important point is that the worst cases

drop off the radar after surgery. When surgery does not work, they give up and are lost to follow-up. Some stop their hormones and live in a limbo between male and female. Others soldier on the best they can in life.

You may say this is speculative. How can I know there is a group of transsexuals living in the shadows, miserable? For one, they will occasionally surface on the internet or in a biography. For instance, Gregory Hemingway, a son of author Ernest Hemingway, had sexual reassignment surgery at age 64 and began using the name Gloria. Yet his public persona fluctuated. He remarried his fourth wife. Sometimes he was seen dressed as a woman. At other times he appeared at a local tavern as "one of the guys." He had breast implant surgery on one breast, then had it reversed. A few days before his death he was arrested for indecent exposure. He first told the police he was Greg, then said he was Gloria. At the time of his death he was in Miami-Dade Woman's Detention center. His life was marred by substance abuse and mental illness. He lost his medical license at 57 for alcoholism. Given his back and forth behavior, it does not seem surgery cured Mr. Hemingway's gender issues, nor did it fix his psychiatric problems. (source: Wikipedia article on Gregory Hemingway, retrieved 8/28/16).

In 2013 Nathan Verhelst, age 44, was put to death under Belgium's euthanasia law. He had been born Nancy but felt unloved as a woman. In 2009 he began hormone therapy and in 2012 had sexual reassignment surgery. But he was unsatisfied with the results, saying: "I was ready to celebrate my new birth. But when I looked in the mirror, I was disgusted with myself. My new breasts did not match my expectations and my new penis had symptoms of rejection. I do not want to be a monster." Hours later he was dead.

(Hamilton, G. November 22, 2013 National Post).

Further details reveal that he had suffered from psychological pain all his life, and the imperfect results of his surgery, the failure of it to live up to his magical expectations, led to his severe depression and death. In my opinion, he should never have been given the surgery. He desperately needed intensive high quality psychotherapy. Instead he was mutilated. When that made him depressed, instead of getting quality psychiatric treatment, he was given a few months of "therapy" before being executed.

Belgium's application of its euthanasia law to people who have depression, rather than actually providing high quality treatment for that depression, is reminiscent of Nazi Germany. Part of the problem is that the people who make the decisions often do not have the training to look inside someone's mind to understand what is going on. For instance Wim Distelmans, the physician who oversaw Mr. Verhelst's case, is Belgium's leading doctor of death. He is an oncologist. In other words, he treats cancer. If he had any training in psychiatry, it was long ago for a month or two in medical school. He is about as qualified as a janitor to determine if someone with depression has exhausted all their treatment options.

The same can be said for most of the doctors involved in the hormonal and surgical treatment of transsexualism. A mental health evaluation may be required in some cases to get in the door, but these are generally cursory at best. Transsexuals resist psychiatric intervention because they don't want to give up the magic hope surgery represents, and they don't want to confront their inner demons in therapy, which is the same logic substance abusers use. The surgeons and endocrinologists who treat these psychiatric cases have had virtually no psychiatric training and do not know how to access the psychological data that is relevant to the individuals they treat. Yet they are given the power to authorize hormones and surgery because they are physicians. And because surgeons are held in such high esteem by our society relative to most other physicians, their expertise is not questioned. It should be.

Walt Heyer is a man who had sexual reassignment surgery and lived as a woman for years before realizing he made a mistake and reversing (as much as was possible) the changes to resume life as a male. He has written several books about his experience and has two websites. (sexchangeregret.com).

The more I looked online, the more cases I found. The failures who show themselves to the public (and there is every reason to think they would avoid public scrutiny) should cause one to take the claims of the proponents of surgery and hormones with a grain of salt. The simple fact is that we do not know if surgery works in the long run or is preferable to psychological treatment because the right kind of studies have not been done. Those studies are randomized controlled trials. They simply do not exist for hormone treatment or sexual reassignment surgery. Neither do they exist for psychotherapy, but the burden of proof should be higher for a treatment that involves cutting off body parts and sexual sterilization than for one that is all talk (or in the case of young children, play). In addition, psychoanalytic psychotherapy allows me to report on what I know from looking through my "microscope": the psychological elements from which gender identify is forged can be seen clearly in the 2 to 5 year-old, as can the forces that drive the process. I have positive evidence of what I am describing; the surgeons do not.

Psychological and Behavioral Treatments

The psychological approaches to gender dysphoria vary depending on age, openness to working on changing gender identity, and many other factors. Below the age of six, gender is still malleable, and the goal should be helping the child accept the body they were born with rather than having society accept them. This can save their future fertility, years of peer-relationship problems, and a lifetime of internal distress. Unfortunately, many parents have been brainwashed by the media into believing gender is fixed at birth; they are afraid of harming their child by any insistence on dress or behavior consistent with the child's sex. They feel trapped into going with the flow and allowing their child to lead.

This, of course, is nonsense. We don't allow our children to choose not to go to school, to refuse vaccinations, to eat ice cream for breakfast, to have any toy they want. However, it may help such parents to know that psychoanalytic psychotherapy is by design non-directive. That is, the therapist has been trained to follow the child's lead whether in talk or play, mainly helping to draw out feelings and thoughts the child may not have communicated to anyone else, helping clarify those feelings and thoughts, and providing enough emotional support during sessions that the child can better deal with their inner stress. Since most gender disorder issues are created by underlying conflicts around other issues, such as attachment, separation anxiety, fear of retaliation, power, and rivalry, it is possible to fix a gender identity disorder without ever talking about gender at all.

Childhood

For children under six, therapy typically involves a combination of play and talk. There are two types of talk used: talking directly about real life on the one hand, or "staying within the metaphor" on the other. Staying within the metaphor means the important issues in the child's life are addressed exclusively through the play characters. Although it might seem to us as adults that this would not be as effective as talking directly about issues, it can be. Young children are creating their inner world through pretend play. The line between reality and imagination is barely visible, which is one reason imaginative play can be so helpful.

As children get older, their sense of self in general, and their gendered self in particular, becomes stiffer, less flexible. However, the underlying psychological issues that helped create gender confusion can still be ameliorated. If this is done, then other options beside hormones and surgery can be found to help the child deal with gender dysphoria.

In many cases of psychotherapy in general, the salutary effect is not a result of directly repairing a broken part of the self, nor is it the result of cutting out pathological fantasies or memories; rather, change in psychotherapy is often brought about by altering the relative balance of competing forces inside the patient's mind. Everyone has both male and female gender identifications on some level. By encouraging the development of same sex gender identifications, the scales may swing to a healthier adaptation. That does not mean cross gender feelings are gone, just that they are less influential in the total personality. Later in life they may come out in sex play between husband and wife rather than in castration and mutilation.

Besides individual psychotherapy, helping children with gender disorders involves working with parents. This can include identifying ways the parents may inadvertently, or on purpose, encourage cross gender identifications and getting them to stop doing that. It may involve suggestions to increase their child's social circle to include more same-sex peers with similar temperaments. It may mean giving parents permission to reward same gender play at the expense of cross gender play.

Some people object to the idea of taking away a boy's dresses, for instance. They see it as too harsh. I wonder if these same parents are reluctant to ground their children from the car or phone privileges when needed. Will they just let their teenagers keep driving after being caught with alcohol, or let them continue using the phone after text-bullying someone at school? Will they be able to enforce any rule, any limit, any consequence?

But perhaps those parents are reacting to what they rightly perceive as confusion or illness in their child and do not want to punish for what can't be helped. Yet if a child has diabetes, he can't have cake, no matter how much he cries for it. Still, in this case there is a middle path that will work better with some children than simply throwing out all the dresses. That is to go through a series of transitions to reach the desired goal while engaging in therapy. For instance, the boy might be given a kilt while the dresses are put up. He would only wear it during certain times and would gradually learn that it is a male, not female garment. Once he learned that, he may well resist wearing it further, which would provide something to talk about in therapy.

Another way of dealing with the boy who wants to

wear dresses is to reward him every time he does not wear a dress. In this way the focus is on positive reinforcement rather than privation. When he puts on a dress to play, he would not be given any extra attention other than what he needed to survive (he would still get to eat dinner, for instance), but when he takes off the dress and agrees to wear pants and a shirt, even if that shirt looks a bit girly, he is given extra attention. After he is no longer wearing dresses the focus can change to having him wear less girly shirts. In subtle but consistent ways the child must hear that although he might at times play at being a girl, he is a boy.

The importance of therapy both for the child and to help the parents cannot be overstated. Gender identity problems arise from a complex mixture of forces that are largely unconscious. They are unlikely to change simply by the parents willing it to. In the beginning of treatment it is common to meet with the therapist several times a week. After the symptoms begin to subside, therapy may be cut back to once a week. Therapy needs to be continued for a time after all symptoms have remitted to consolidate the gains made. Then there may be periodical checks once a year throughout development to look for any signs of relapse.

Older children may have spent so much time practicing at being the other sex that they do not know how to be their own. In that case they might benefit from coaching on "how to be a boy" or "how to be a girl." This is only possible if the child likes the person who is coaching them, and if the child is willing to try. The better the relationship between patient and therapist, the more likely this will succeed. This kind of coaching may be essential in helping an older child or teenager improve.

For psychotherapy of any kind to work, the most important ingredient is the relationship between the therapist and patient. For instance, one little girl who desperately wanted to be a boy responded to overtures to expand her horizons by suggesting her therapist dress as a girl. He said he would if she would. They had a great dress-up session that allowed her to practice being a girl and to imagine herself as one while having fun at the same time.

There are plenty of detailed case reports of success in resolving gender confusion through psychoanalytic psychotherapy. Each case is unique, depending on the individual psychological factors. Each can only be understood by looking through the microscope that psychoanalytic psychotherapy provides.

Adolescence

As children reach puberty and begin to feel their bodies change, they often get desperate to change sex. This can bring on suicidal feelings. The solution is not to jump to the knife. As I mentioned, adolescence is all about the body changing and the teen adapting. Teenagers with gender dysphoria will need a lot of extra support, including at times inpatient hospitalization, in order to help them contain their confusing and powerful feelings. I do not recommend puberty blockers. A principal argument for blockers are that they allow a time of puberty moratorium, which supposedly buys time for the teenager to work through gender issues. But without the pressure of same sex hormones, teenage transsexuals have little motivation to do anything but wait until they are old enough for surgery, and the numbers support this. Once on the hormone and surgery train, virtually no teenager leaves it.

The other main argument in support of puberty blockers is that they cut down on the need for more surgery, such as later having to shave down an Adam's apple or soften a chin, as if these touch-up surgeries compare at all to hacking someone's genitals off and removing their internal sexual organs. This is not enough of an argument to counterbalance the therapeutic possibility of changing psychological gender identity in the context of psychotherapy. If there is no movement after a couple of years of first rate psychotherapy, then whatever nascent changes have occurred under the influence of the body's own hormones can be reversed if no other option is possible.

But there are almost always other options. Some gender disordered teenagers who are not able to fully return to their biological gender psychologically are able to find a resolution by accepting a homosexual lifestyle. While this has its own problems (loss of a chance for biological children, especially among males, increased risk of many diseases, including psychological ones), it is a lot better than being hacked to pieces and put back together like the Bride of Frankenstein.

Finally, teenagers might be encouraged to live like transgender individuals did in the days before hormones and surgery – play dress-up.

So how well do these psychological treatments work? As I mentioned, the younger the child the better the results. As gender identity becomes more a core part of the self, changing it becomes a bigger project. Nevertheless, there are case reports of curing teenage transsexualism. (Kronberg, 1981; Barlow, 1973; Davenport, 1977). For instance, Davenport describes the the inpatient treatment of a 14 year-old girl who told her parents she wanted a sex change operation when she was 12. At the time of admission she was refusing to wear girl's clothes, was withdrawn from her peers, and her academic performance was tanking. "The patient convincingly presented herself as a boy in dress, voice, movement, interests, and orientation." In a letter to her psychiatrist she said: "I want to be a boy more than anything in the world." She had felt like a boy since at least second grade and would fight with her mother over wearing slacks (her mother wanted her to wear a dress) in nursery school. During the evaluation she insisted on having sexual reassignment surgery, not concerned with how many operations it might take. Then, she said, "I could start living a normal boy's life."

If you read any of the online accounts by other transsexuals, this will all be familiar. The impression of the staff at the hospital was: "the most striking thing about her was her male presentation.... Her interests were traditionally masculine and her uninterest in feminine activities was obvious. She would respond with delight when someone referred to her as a boy and with anger or embarrassment when referred to as a girl." The patient had a classic case of transsexualism.

The therapy was difficult, made so in part by her "severe constriction of thought. She had a hard time elaborating on any idea...." But the therapist and staff were patient, and over time she began to address issues, first concerning her family relationships, then her magical belief surgery could change her into a boy. When she found that the surgery would not allow her to become a father, to have natural children as a man, that began to turn the tide.

Over time she became less sure she was a boy

trapped in a girl's body. She questioned her identity. Several events in her family allowed her to feel proud of her mother and began an identification process with her mother, and hence with women in general. During her two-year hospitalization she dealt with many issues that all fed into her gender dysphoria. As she dealt with them, her dysphoria gradually dissipated. She left the hospital no longer gender dysphoric, appearing every bit a young woman. She had taken an interest in babysitting. Follow-up two and a half years later revealed that she continued "to dress in a most feminine manner and appears to have adopted a feminine identity." She was 19, in college, and alluded to an interest in boys.

It is worth noting that in the three cases I referenced the teenagers not only lost their gender dysphoria, they became emotionally healthier in a number of other ways as well. The bad news is that the treatments required 1-2 years of inpatient hospitalization, which I consider a modest price to pay for a normal life free of surgery and the infertility it imposes, but something our current healthcare system will not pay for.

We can expect that as politics and a broken psychiatric system have closed down a viable form of psychological treatment for adolescent gender dysphoria – long term inpatient hospitalization – and that as the surgeons and endocrinologists continue to push the age limit lower for somatic treatment, more and more people will have surgery with all the complications that entails and will miss out on the more appropriate psychiatric treatment. Further, as prepubertal children are put on hormone blockers, they will miss out on the brain changes that occur during adolescence and the opportunity to overcome their gender dysphoria on their own.

Rupert Everett, an actor, in an interview with the Sunday Times in June of 2016 cautioned against sex change operations, remarking that since early childhood he wanted to be a girl and dressed exclusively as one for a time. He told the Sunday Times magazine: "I really wanted to be a girl. Thank God the world of now wasn't then, because I'd be on hormones and I'd be a woman. After I was 15 I never wanted to be a woman again." My guess is that was the age when he came to terms with his homosexual feelings, allowing him to change his self-image from female to gay male. That saved him from hormones and surgery.

The natural history of early gender dysphoria is that a substantial proportion of these children resolve their gender issues (at least on the surface) and become homosexual. That seems a better alternative than castration. But the more the magical fantasy of surgery is promoted, the more castration and surgical mutilation occur.

Chapter 5: Prevention

An ounce of prevention is worth a pound of cure. In the case of gender dysphoria, that means intervening as soon as problems are evident. Unfortunately, many people are told by their physicians that cross-gendered behavior is probably just a phase. A couple of years go by during which the child's confusion over his or her gender is left to grow and become more entrenched. But should every two-year-old boy who tries on his mother's high heels be referred for evaluation?

As I mentioned earlier, boys and girls develop identifications with both their parents. It is normal for a boy to try on his mother's shoes and for a girl to imitate her father on occasion. Children play at many things while they grow up. Their pretend play is essential for the development of their sense of self. It is not the individual behaviors but the pattern, intensity, and persistence that suggest a problem needing investigation.

Although normal children may sporadically play at being the opposite gender, their play feels playful. Children with gender dysphoria don't seem to be having fun so much as being compelled to behave like the opposite sex. They may say they are the opposite sex or will change sex when they grow up. Normal children will easily put down the dress-up clothes when asked, while a boy with gender confusion will throw a tantrum rather than take off a dress. A boy may play dolls with his sisters because he wants to play with his sisters. But he usually does not play with Barbie dolls by himself, at least not for extended periods or at the exclusion of more typical boy toys.

Normal children are comfortable being boys and girls. They are usually quick to correct adults who call them by the wrong gender. Children with gender dysphoria don't like being the sex they are. They not only play at being the opposite sex, they actively avoid doing anything associated with their biological sex. Boys with gender problems may want to get rid of their penises while girls with gender problems want one.

Although it is normal for children to play act at being dogs, cats, superheroes, and the opposite sex, such play is easy to pick out as "just play." Children with gender dysphoria don't let up on their insistence they are the opposite sex. They seem stuck on this one topic. They try to act like the opposite sex, look like the opposite sex, and want to be addressed as the opposite sex. It is pervasive.

Although it is true that mild gender confusion in young children often remits, the more rigid, the more pervasive, and the more intense the symptoms, the less likely they are to go away on their own. Hence, although a parent need not be alarmed if her son occasionally tries on her shoes or plays with his sister's dolls as long as he is also playing with his trucks and trying to imitate his father, that parent should be concerned if her son seems to want nothing to do with his father or boy's toys, calls himself a girl, and insists on wearing a dress. In the latter case, it is better to get him in to be evaluated within a couple of months of the behavior appearing.

If a child with gender dysphoria is brought into therapy under the age of five, the chance of cure is very high. In that way years of hormones, multiple surgeries, infertility, and peer ostracism can all be prevented. If too much time is allowed to pass, however, the child becomes harder to influence and cure is not as certain.

Between the two examples I gave, one of a child who occasionally plays with opposite sex toys or clothes and that of the child who is rigidly fixated on being the opposite sex and hates his or her own gender, there are a number of children who are harder to classify. These include the feminine boys who avoid rough and tumble play, other boys, and prefer to be by their mother's side or playing with girls. Because of greater contact with girls and women, they may take on more of the characteristics of females and may not know how to relate to other boys as a boy. Even if this kind of boy does not ever want a sex change, he is still at risk for peer ostracism, at least by other boys. He is also at risk for some gender confusion as he tries to find his place in the world. This can lead to chronic stress, lower in intensity than with full-blown gender dysphoria, but still not good for development.

Sometimes boys like I described are born with a sensitive temperament that causes them to shy away from the rough and tumble play typical of boys. They can be helped a great deal if their parents find male playmates for them of similar temperament. They might also be enrolled in specific clubs or groups where such children are likely to be found, such as art camp, music camp, or computer camp. The father can be particularly helpful if he adjusts his behaviors and interactions to match his son's temperament.

Similarly with girls who are naturally more rough and tumble than their classmates, who may drive other girls away with their high activity level. They may enjoy playing only with boys, which can lead to chronic stress and low-grade confusion. Tomboys are not usually subject to quite the same peer ridicule as feminine boys, though it can be just as bad when puberty hits. Again, pairing with similar girls may be helpful. Activities that can focus their energy in an appropriate gender based way include gymnastics, girl scouts, dance, and sports.

I think we all would like our children to learn to accept themselves for who they are. Gender dysphoria interferes with that. The only reasonable treatment at a young age is a combination of individual psychotherapy and family guidance. Failure to provide that multiplies the child's suffering and extends it over years or for a lifetime.

Chapter 6: Politics, Culture, Madness

In this country and others transsexual political power has grown far beyond its original base. Playing on the American ideals of fairness and equality, transgender activists have worked hard to make gender identity a civil rights rather than medical issue. They have succeeded beyond what anyone even a few years ago could have imagined. Building on the success of banning conversion therapy for homosexuals in California, they worked hard to extend such bans to treating children with gender dysphoria. Arguing that children cannot consent to treatment (ignoring that children do not consent to any medical treatment; it is only parents who can give consent for a minor), they created the greatest impediment to helping gender dysphoric children in the state. They have condemned thousands of children to peer rejection, depression, anxiety, loss of fertility, unnecessary surgery, hormone treatments, and suicide. As I pointed out in the last section, the best way to deal with gender confusion is through early treatment, and they made that virtually impossible. Any therapist in California who admits to trying to help "convert" a gender dysphoric four-year-old child into accepting their birth sex opens him or herself up to a lawsuit as well as possible legal action.

At the time of this writing, the ban against conversion therapy has spread to Vermont, New Jersey, Illinois, Oregon, the District of Columbia, and Cincinnati. More are sure to follow. This is a gross overstepping of the government and ensures many more children will grow up to be plagued by transsexual feelings.

One of the reasons that these bills pass is that legislators are presented with worst case scenarios. Tales of people who were subject to harsh, punitive treatment and aversive conditioning in an attempt to change them as teenagers, for instance. The suicide note of a transgender teen who killed herself is often read. In the note she blames the people who tried to change her back to being a boy. No one brings up the professional therapists who play with young children and recommend nothing more harsh than having the parents gradually wean their children away from cross-gender toys and dress. No one discusses the damage caused by not allowing early intervention.

Part of the problem is that conversion therapy has often been based at religious institutions. Unrealistic expectations of change through prayer and acts of penance have not helped public opinion of conversion therapy. Totally absent to the public eye is the work done by psychoanalytic therapists behind closed doors one patient at a time. It would have been better to limit conversion therapy to doctoral level mental health professionals than to ban it entirely.

There is a real risk that at some time the misguided left will gain enough power to make a federal law banning conversion therapy. Then what help will there be for confused children and adolescents? Only surgery. Sometimes I wonder if this is the plan of the transgender community who, after all, lacks the capacity to reproduce any other way. To them, converting someone away from transsexualism weakens their political power.

What To Do

One thing you can do is write you local, state, and national representatives and ask them not to limit therapy designed to help children and adolescents with sexual and gender problems. The only reasonable limit would be restricting the therapy to mental health professionals who are licensed by the state. Churches can serve supportive functions, but the therapy needs to be directed and delivered by mental health providers. The problem of unscrupulous or abusive providers would be handled the same way as with any similar problem – through the state medical, psychology, and counseling boards and through the civil legal system.

Without continued attempts to change psychological gender identity to match physical sex no new treatments will be tried or created. Whatever limitations that exist today may be overcome through continued effort. There was a time when a diagnosis of cancer meant certain death. This is not true now. Many cancers are curable, others can be kept at bay for years. The same can be said of many diseases. What would the world be like if we had tied doctors' hands back then?

We must allow continued treatment of gender dysphoria from all angles while we actively research the effectiveness of those treatments. Many people have argued that it is not ethical to randomize adults with gender dysphoria who want surgery into a group that gets surgery and a group that does not. I would argue that it is not ethical to continue butchering humanity without good evidence that it really works, and the only way to get that clear evidence is through a number of randomized controlled trials with lengthy follow-up periods. I believe the real reason those people oppose such studies is that they fear the results. After all, the only good long-term follow-up study showed a 19-fold increase in suicide relative to the general population.

Although I believe we already have strong data supporting the use of psychotherapy to change pathological gender identifications, it would help convince those people who do not have the benefit of being able to directly view the psychodynamic processes in the minds of young children if we also had some randomized controlled trials of psychotherapy in young children. This cannot happen, however, if such therapy is banned.

Since the data for sexual reassignment surgery is no better than for psychotherapy, and the risks are much worse, it does not make sense that health insurance companies be compelled to pay for surgery and hormone therapy. Rather, given the psychoanalytic data supporting psychological treatment, especially for young children, and the relative lack of risk plus the advantage of helping treat the many psychiatric comorbidities associated with gender dysphoria, it makes sense that health insurance fund such treatment fully, including extended residential care for adolescents. Finally, research grants need to be made available to test all potential therapies.

Chapter 7: Conclusion

I started this booklet by pointing out the craziness of cutting off our most intimate parts as a treatment for a psychiatric problem. It just does not make common sense. Yet it is the accepted treatment for gender confusion. In trying to understand this, we asked several important questions: Is there any evidence sexual reassignment surgery and cross-gender hormone treatments work? Is there any evidence psychological treatments work? And are we ignoring more fundamental problems, problems that lead to suicide later in life by focusing so much on changing the appearance of gender?

To answer those questions we first had to identify the underlying assumptions the transgender community holds. One is that psychological gender is biologically fixed at birth. We demonstrated that there is no evidence to support this. In the cases where people have had documented hormone imbalances in utero and in early life we may see differences in activity level and rough and tumble play, but the majority of such children do not have gender dysphoria. And there is no evidence for any such hormonal derangement in transsexuals to begin with.

Another assumption is that a person can change sex. That is impossible. Unfortunately, the magical belief that surgery can change a person's fundamental gender draws people away from getting real help through psychotherapy.

As of this writing, there is no evidence that sexual reassignment surgery and hormone therapy works in the long run. There is only one well done 10-year follow-up study in existence, and that showed horrible psychological results with a 19-fold increased rate of suicide compared to the normal population. There is plenty of evidence that gender dysphoria can remit in young children engaged in psychotherapy, and that the remission holds into adulthood. Because of the nature of psychoanalytic psychotherapy, it has been possible to gain further validity by documenting the psychological changes that correspond with remission of gender confusion. Finally, there are some cases of adolescents who have been successfully treated, though the follow-up data are not ideal.

There is no doubt we could benefit from more research, especially from randomized controlled trials, but at this point the data clearly supports early childhood psychological intervention as the best hope for the treatment of gender dysphoria and the prevention of extensive psychiatric and physical comorbidity. Surgery and hormones do nothing to treat the fundamental disorders of the self that people with gender dysphoria suffer from. Focusing on changing appearance neglects the very real psychiatric needs of these patients and feeds a magical fantasy that encourages the patients to avoid getting any psychiatric help. Worst of all, surgery leaves the individual mutilated, infertile, and scarred for life. Psychoanalytically informed play with children and gentle encouragement of gender appropriate play offers much more potential benefit and essentially no risk.

If you have a child who is suffering from gender dysphoria, I encourage you to take him or her to a child psychoanalyst, child psychiatrist, or another child therapist who is well trained in the psychoanalytic or psychodynamic psychotherapy of young children. Other child therapists may be able to help if they have a talent for working with children, are open minded, and are willing to get supervision from an expert. If the first professional you find has been brainwashed about the magic power of surgery, find another and get a second opinion. Don't mindlessly castrate your child.

References

Barlow, D., Reynolds, J., Agras, S. (1973). "Gender Identity Change in a Transsexual." Archives of General Psychiatry. Vol 28, pp 569-576. April 1973.

Bizic, M., et al. (2014). "An Overview of Neovaginal Reconstruction Options in Male to Female Transsexuals." The Scientific World Journal. Vol 2014 (2014), Article ID 638919, 8 pages. DOI: 10.1155/2014/638919

Chung WC, De Vries GJ, Swaab DF. (2002). "Sexual differentiation of the bed nucleus of the stria terminalis in humans may extend into adulthood." J Neurosci. 2002;22:1027–1033.

Davenport, C., Harrison, S. (1977). "Gender Identity Change in a Female Adolescent Transsexual." Arch Sex Behav.1977 Jul;6(4):327-40. PMID:889433

Dessens, A., Slijper, F., Drop, S. (2005). "Gender Dysphoria and Gender Change in Chromosomal Females with Congenital Adrenal Hyperplasia." Archives of Sexual Behavior, Vol. 34, No. 4. August 2005. DOI: 10.1007/s10508-005-4338-5.

de Vries, A., Steensma, T., Doreleijers, T., Cohen-Kettenis, P. (2011). "Puberty Suppression in Adolescents With Gender Identity Disorder: A Prospective Follow-Up Study." J Sex Med 2011;8:2276–2283. DOI: 10.1111/j.1743-6109.2010.01943.x

Dhejne C, Lichtenstein P, Boman M, Johansson ALV, Langstrom N, et al. (2011) "Long-Term Follow-Up of Transsexual Persons Undergoing Sex Reassignment Surgery: Cohort Study in Sweden." PLoS ONE 6(2): e16885. doi:10.1371/journal.pone.0016885

Dhejne, C., Oberg, K., Arver, S., Landen, M. (2014). "An Analysis of All Applications for Sex Reassignment Surgery in Sweden, 1960–2010: Prevalence, Incidence, and Regrets." Archives of Sexual Behavior. DOI 10.1007/s10508-014-0300-8

Flores, A., Herman, J., Gates, G., Brown, T. (2016). "How many adults identify as transgender in the united states?" The Williams Institute, UCLA School of Law. June 2016.

Gates, G. (2011) "How many people are lesbian, gay, bisexual, and transgender?" The Williams Institute, UCLA School of Law. April 2011.

Hamilton, G. November 22, 2013. National Post.

http://news.nationalpost.com/news/canada/termi-nally-transsexual-concerns-raised-over-belgian-euth-anized-after-botched-sex-change   Retrieved 8/18/2016

Hepp, U., Kraemer, B., Schnyder, U., Miller, N., Del-signore, A. (2005). "Psychiatric comorbidity in gen-der identity disorder." Journal of Psychosomatic Re-search 58 (2005) 259– 261. doi:10.1016/j.jpsy-chores.2004.08.010

Heylens, G., De Cuypere, G., Zucker, K., Schelfaut, C., Elaut, E., Bossche, H., De Baere, E., T'Sjoen, G. (2012). "Gender Identity Disorder in Twins: A Review of the Case Report Literature. J Sex Med 2012;9:751–757. DOI: 10.1111/j.1743-6109.2011.02567.x.

Joel, D., Berman Z., Tavorc, I., Wexlerd, N., Gabera, O., Steind, Y., Shefia,N., Poole, J., Urchse, S., Mar-guliese, D., Lieme,F., Hänggif, J., Jänckef, L., and As-safb, Y. (2015) "Sex beyond the genitalia: The human brain mosaic." PNAS, Vol. 112, No. 50, December 2015.   pp   15468-15473.   DOI 10.1073/pnas.1509654112.

Kohut, H. (1959). "Introspection, empathy, and psychoanalysis: an examination of the relationship between mode of observation and theory." Journal of the American Psychoanalytic Association, Vol 7, Jul 1959, 459-483.

Kohut, H. (1977). The Restoration of the Self. New York: International Universities Press.

Kronberg, J., Tyano, S., Apter, A, Wijsenbeek, H. (1981) "Treatment of transsexualism in adolescence."

Journal of Adolescence, 1981, 4, 177-185. DOI: 10.1016/S0140-1971(81)80037-1

Lawrence, A. (2008). "Gender Identity Disorders in Adults: Diagnosis and Treatment" in Handbook of Sexual and Gender Identity Disorders, Ed. David L. Rowland and Luca Incrocci. John Wiley & Sons, Inc.

Meyer-Bhalburg, H. (2005). "Gender Identity Outcome in Female-Raised 46,XY Persons with Penile Agenesis, Cloacal Exstrophy of the Bladder, or Penile Ablation." Archives of Sexual Behavior, Vol. 34, No. 4, August 2005. pp 423-438. DOI: 10.1007/s10508-005-4342-9.

Woollett, K., Maguire, E. (2011). "Acquiring 'The Knowledge' of London's Layout Drives Structural Brain Changes." Current Biology Vol 21 No 24. December 2011. pp 2109-2114. DOI 10.1016/j.cub.2011.11.018

Zucker, J. (2014). "Gender Dysphoria." in Lewis, M., and Rudolph, K.D. (eds.), Handbook of Developmental Psychopathology, DOI 10.1007/978-1-4614-9608-3_35, Springer Science+Business Media New York 2014.

https://www.theguardian.com/film/2016/jun/19/ruperteverettdangersofchildsexchangeoperations-gender.